The Complementary PHP Testing Tools Cookbook

by Chris Hartjes

php[architect] print edition

The Complementary PHP Testing Tools Cookbook

php[architect] edition published: May 2020

Print ISBN:	978-1-957147-00-0
PDF ISBN:	978-1-957147-01-7
ePub ISBN:	978-1-957147-02-4
Kindle ISBN	978-1-957147-03-1

Produced & Printed in the United States

Disclaimer

Written by
Chris Hartjes

Editor
Kara Ferguson

Layout
John Congdon

Published by
PHP Architect, LLC.
9245 Twin Trails Dr #720503
San Diego, CA 92129 USA

406-PHP-ARCH (406-747-2724)
info@phparch.com
www.phparch.com

Table of Contents

Foreword by Marco Pivetta

(Marco is a long-time and prolific contributor to Open Source PHP projects. I've been lucky enough to work with Marco for several years and I learn how to do something better almost every single time we go a code review or have a discussion surrounding software development. I asked him to take a look at this book and reflect on the changes he has seen in the PHP development community in the decade we've known each other.)

I've known Chris, the "grumpy programmer", since almost a decade now: he and I share most of our views around how teams should keep control over software complexity and stability.

His long career around software testing, automation tooling and general betterment of developers that he managed to reach is showing its impact over our industry: a decade ago, testing was looked upon with skepticism within the PHP ecosystem, sometimes even frown upon, "an expensive exercise".

Where there was skepticism, there is now clear interest in testing on many levels, and the discussion shifted from "should I write tests?" to "what are the best testing techniques?".

The community at large has clearly adopted software testing, and so probably have you, since you are reading this book.

The next step lies in understanding whether our tests are good, are verifying all the important details of our projects, and whether we are writing code that is to the point. We want to avoid useless complexity, embracing brevity, and improve expressiveness of our work, to the benefit of ourselves and our peers.

As a code-quality evangelist myself, I suggest you to try the tools and techniques presented in the next chapters, make them your own.

You will learn about practices that I personally made part of my own daily engineering work, and they will have a deep impact on how you write software.

By mixing and leveraging them, you may be able to find your level of comfort in code quality, as well as the knowledge needed to convince others about their value.

Chapter 1

Getting Started

Audience

The topic of testing is tough to explain to people who are just learning to program. "I'm going to write code that tests other code I write? That seems really hard!" I have yet to see a tutorial that teaches programmers how to use a programming language from a test-centric position.

With that in mind, I wrote this book for PHP programmers who already have experience writing tests but want to improve. I have been doing this since 2005 and still go through the process of learning new things and reinforcing older habits that can lead to better outcomes.

My book "The Grumpy Programmer's Guide To Testing PHP Applications" (available via LeanPub[1] or php|architect[2]) goes over the basic technical and core skills you need to learn, and hopefully master, to make your tests effective and turn writing tests into just something you do instead of a rare event.

---

[1] https://leanpub.com/grumpy-guide
[2] https://phpa.me/grumpy-testing-book

Throughout this book, I am going to show you how I am adding targeted test coverage to my oldest, still-in-use PHP-based web application. It has been running since 2004, with me updating the base framework (CakePHP[3]) every few years.

Why Make All This Effort?

The application began as a PHP 5 codebase and has been updated over the years. It now runs fine on PHP 7.4 and hopefully PHP 8.0 soon. It's extremely rare in the current phase of the software industry to work on an application for so long. The skillset needed to build something from scratch, and the skillset needed to maintain an existing codebase are quite different! I believe that more and more developers understanding this has led to all these great tools available in multiple languages, making testing and code analysis easier.

After all, if you're going to build something and never touch it again after deployment, then you probably have no need for automated tests and code linting and static analysis. However, if you are building something that is going to be the long-lived core of a business or project, it is worth exploring automated testing, code linting, and static code analysis to find out how they can help you.

The Application

The application itself is a website for a league that uses a tabletop baseball simulation game to play out a full season using rosters made up of players from existing Major League Baseball teams. We make the game ourselves and distribute it to league members and other interested parties for free.

When it comes to verifying the application is behaving as expected, some of the things that can be visually confirmed are:

- league standings
- scheduled games
- pitching rotations teams will use
- injuries

To be perfectly clear–knowledge of the sport of baseball is not a requirement to understand the approach I am using in this book! It certainly helps, but the key point I want to emphasize is that without some domain knowledge of the problem you are trying to solve you might create tests that have no impact.

---

[3] https://cakephp.org

For a various reasons, mostly related to the concept of "the prototype becomes production," we have no test coverage. Typically, this would be a massive problem for any website people frequently use, but I am a "domain expert" for the problem we are solving. This allows me to make very lazy shortcuts and visually verify things work as expected.

Chances are, if you are joining a project and dealing with a long-lived legacy application it's very likely you do not have the same level of knowledge of both the application's code and the problem it's solving. Because of my knowledge, I can skip a whole category of automated tests where the output of various pages is compared to a baseline. Manually reloading pages after making small changes is not a great practice. Still, at this point, it is highly unlikely that writing a series of automated tests will give us a sense of confidence about the deployments we need. No other developers are likely to join the "team" to work on it. I know enough to visually confirm if things are working as expected.

Still, no tests? Yes, to my great personal shame, it is a huge oversight that now needs to be corrected. Every year when we tweak things and ready the website to cover the upcoming season, a few things break. Because I understand how EVERYTHING is supposed to work, these are quick changes. It would be nice to get to the point where all the things that break happen before I push the changes into production.

So why am I bothering to add automated tests, given that some types of tests are likely not to help? That domain knowledge often leads me to forget to check that everything works instead of only visually checking the one thing I changed.

By adding tests that cover the things that have to work whenever updated code is deployed into production I am trying to change the cycle of:

- make local changes
- imperfectly test local changes
- push changes to production
- get email from people that "something is broken"

The price of failure here is pretty low–it's a website supporting a hobby. Any urgency I feel is created by myself; chances are your own situation is much different. Bugs or unexpected behavior in your web applications can lead to losing money, losing jobs, or could even damage the business behind it.

I am a firm believer in getting a computer to do repeatable tasks for you. As humans, we make mistakes. We skip steps. We assume the state of things. Computers only follow the instructions we give them. Hopefully, those instructions match how we believe things should behave.

Using automated tools is often like having another person on your team tirelessly checking your work for mistakes and making suggestions on what to change. Who doesn't want help like that?

Our Tools

As of this writing (spring and summer 2021), I have the following tools installed; they are used throughout this book.

- PHP 7.4 and PHP 8.0
- PHPStan 0.12.85
- Infection 0.21.0
- PHPUnit 8.5.1
- PostgreSQL 9.6

I am doing this work on macOS Big Sur 11.3 and have used Homebrew[4] to install most of the dependencies I need.

I am also using PhpStorm[5] as my editor, which has great integration with all three of the test-centric tools along with the PHP Extended Inspections[6] extension, which makes lots of refactoring suggestions and reminders about things like uninitialized variables.

Before I go any further, I want to remind you that my choice of tools is just that: my choice of tools. There are many other options for each type of tool I am using, and I am a strong believer in not using tools that cause you any friction. If you want to use PHPStan[7] for static code analysis, go ahead! If you want to skip doing mutation testing, that's cool too. Don't like PHPUnit's syntax and want to use something like Pest[8]? Go for it.

The point is to start integrating the use of tools that complement test-centric practices. Your choice of tools won't change what you have to do, but it does influence how you approach it.

---

[4] https://brew.sh/

[5] https://www.jetbrains.com/phpstorm

[6] *https://phpa.me/php-inspections-extended*

[7] https://phpstan.org

[8] https://pestphp.com

Initial Set Up

This book also assumes you are using the tool that I feel changed PHP development forever, Composer[9]. If you are not familiar with it, it is a command line interface tool for installing PHP packages. You will be hard-pressed in 2021 to find a major PHP library or framework that is not using Composer in some way.

Some of the tools I'm using require you to do some configuration work before you can use them.

PHPStan

PHPStan's documentation can be found at https://phpstan.org.

PHPStan can be used without a default configuration file–you just need to pass it information via the CLI. To reduce cognitive load, I'll just create a default `phpstan.neon` file:

```
parameters:
    level: max
    paths:
        - src
        - tests
```

Infection

Infection's documentation can be found at https://infection.github.io.

I chose to install Infection using PHIVE[10].

PHPStan can be used without a default configuration file–you just need to pass it information via the CLI. To reduce cognitive load, I'll just create a default `phpstan.neon` file:

```
parameters:
    level: max
    paths:
        - src
        - tests
```

Infection

Infection's documentation can be found at https://infection.github.io.

---

[9] https://getcomposer.org
[10] https://phar.io/

I chose to install Infection using PHIVE[11]: as there were some Composer issues that I could not properly resolve. The first run of the CLI tool gives you a similar message (some output has been removed).

```
> infection.phar

  Welcome to the Infection config generator



We did not find a configuration file. The following questions will help us to generate it for you.


Which source directories do you want to include (comma separated)? [src]:
  [0 ] .
  [1 ] bin
  [2 ] config
  [3 ] lib
  [4 ] logs
  [5 ] plugins
  [6 ] src
  [7 ] templates
  [8 ] tests
  [9 ] tmp
  [10] vendor
  [11] webroot
 > 6,7

Configuration file "infection.json.dist" was created.
```

I am using the same strategy for the configuration file for this tool as I did with PHPStan. Here's the default configuration file. I'll explain how to tweak it the first time I use it later in the book.

```
{
    "source": {
        "directories": [
            "src",
            "templates"
        ]
```

[11] https://github.com/phar-io/phive

Chapter 2

Static Code Analysis Tooling

What Is It?

I like to introduce programming ideas by sharing a definition from a reliable source. In this case, Wikipedia:

> *Static program analysis is the analysis of computer software that is performed without actually executing programs, in contrast with dynamic analysis, which is analysis performed on programs while they are executing. In most cases the analysis is performed on some version of the source code, and in the other cases, some form of the object code.*

The part of this that intrigued me when I first started looking into it was the "without actually executing programs" part. About a decade ago, I tried creating my own tool that would perform static analysis of PHP code to figure out dependencies and language constructs you needed to test. It quickly led me down a rabbit hole of figuring out how to parse PHP tokens and abstract syntax trees.

In the end, I figured out it was easier to write books and give talks about teaching people to do what my poorly-built tool was trying to do in an automated fashion.

In this book, I am using PHPStan[1] but I have also used Psalm[2] for the same purposes. Other options I am aware of are phan[3] and exakat[4]. However, PHPStan and Psalm are definitely the ones with the most "market share" in PHP.

As a quick summary and to focus the rest of this chapter: static code analysis provides a way of testing your code without having to run it. A static analysis tool can look at your PHP code and infer things about how it should work based on the types associated with your variables, functions, and classes. It can highlight whether you're potentially passing a parameter with an ambiguous type, if you're calling a function in an unexpected way, identify areas of code that will never be executed, and more. As PHP has matured and added features like type hints and strict mode, static analysis tools can give you a better understanding of application code and give more useful feedback.

Why Should I Use It?

When I first started looking at and using these tools, I quickly realized that the high-level purpose was to accurately figure out the intent of the code I was writing.

When parameter typing and return value typing were added to the language, it helped me out in two ways. First, it eliminated a whole category of tests designed to answer questions like, "Did we get an array back?" Once you could say, at the language level, "this variable is supposed to be an integer," then the PHP interpreter could do that test for me.

With the use of types, the static analysis tools could read in my code, parse it, and then start looking at code that is calling it. When I started using these tools, I began to appreciate that I had something looking at what I did and making suggestions:

"I know you are accepting an array as this parameter, but look at how in one place it is given an array of integers, while elsewhere it is an array of mixed values. Which one are you expecting?"

"I noticed that you are calling this method on this object you generated a few lines up. I can't tell what type of object it is supposed to be due to some lazy loading behind the scenes. Can you add an annotation to help me figure it out?"

---

[1] PHPStan
[2] https://psalm.dev
[3] https://github.com/phan/phan
[4] https://exakat.io

I have found this sort of information to be helpful in determining the correct intent of my code. Before the use of type hinting became a common practice in PHP applications, you could provide those hints using documentation blocks[5] but they might not get updated or reflect the current state of the code. Many IDE's can help out by looking at both the documentation blocks and type hints–if you've ever seen someone mention "intellesense" or "code completion," this is likely what they are referring to.

Who Should Be Using It?

Developers should be using static code analysis tools while doing their coding work, hopefully before they attempt to commit their code to their version control system.

If you have some reluctant developers, you could always rely on the commit hooks for your version control system and add it there. My own recommendation is to create it as a pre-commit hook–no commit goes through unless the static analysis tool is happy!

Just remember that any use of a tool like this also needs to be accompanied by code reviews to make sure that some of the techniques you can use to make PHPStan "happy" are being correctly applied.

How Do I Do It?

The configuration file for PHPStan (called `phpstan.neon`) contains the minimal amount of options:

```
parameters:
    bootstrapFiles:
        - config/bootstrap.php
    level: max
    paths:
        - src
        - tests
```

PHPStan's documentation covers these options and more, but I want to talk about the ones I am using.

The framework for this application (CakePHP[6] uses a bootstrap file, so I tell PHPStan to use it so it can see things like framework-related configuration values and any custom values I might be using. Depending on the underlying framework, I might not need this at all.

---

[5] *documentation blocks:* https://docs.phpdoc.org/latest/guide/guides/docblocks.html
[6] *CakePHP:* https://cakephp.org

I can also tell it what paths I want it to scan. I definitely don't want to be doing any analysis of third-party code in the `vendor` directory created by installing packages via Composer.

PHPStan also uses the concept of an "analysis level." This tells PHPStan just how strict to be in its analysis of your code. I went with 'max' (which is an alias for 7) and the range is 0 to 7. By default, it goes with 0. What if I go with level 0?

```
Note: Using configuration file /Users/chartjes/Sites/ibl/phpstan.neon.
 51/51 [████████████████████████████] 100%

 ------ -----------------------------------------------------------------------------------------
  Line   src/Shell/ConsoleShell.php
 ------ -----------------------------------------------------------------------------------------
  60     Method App\Shell\ConsoleShell::main() should return int|null but return statement is missing.
 ------ -----------------------------------------------------------------------------------------
```

Okay, just one error. I should be using return type hints and PHPStan tells me to add one. Once I do that, PHPStan reports no errors.

I continue raising the level until I get a new set of errors. At the second level, I get:

```
Note: Using configuration file /Users/chartjes/Sites/ibl/phpstan.neon.
 51/51 [████████████████████████████] 100%
 ------ ---------------------------------------------------------------------------
  Line   src/Controller/Component/StandingsComponent.php
 ------ ---------------------------------------------------------------------------
  514    Comparison operation ">=" between (array|float|int) and 13 results in an error.
  525    Comparison operation "<=" between (array|float|int) and 5 results in an error.
 ------ ---------------------------------------------------------------------------

 ------ -------------------------------------------------------
  Line   src/Model/Table/GamesTable.php
 ------ -------------------------------------------------------
  143    Call to an undefined method Cake\ORM\Query::orWhere().
 ------ -------------------------------------------------------

 ------ ---------------------------------------------------------------------
  Line   src/Util/Rosters.php
 ------ ---------------------------------------------------------------------
  15     Call to an undefined method Cake\ORM\Table::generateListByNicknameName().
 ------ ---------------------------------------------------------------------

 ------ --------------------------------------------------------
  Line   src/View/AjaxView.php
 ------ --------------------------------------------------------
  48     Call to an undefined method Cake\Http\Response::type().
 ------ --------------------------------------------------------

 [ERROR] Found 5 errors
```

Now it seems like PHPStan is definitely getting stricter and pointing out things in my code that, while it works, could potentially cause problems down the road. A summary of its complaints could be:

1. I need to deliberately cast some values in comparisons.
2. I need to specifically tell PHPStan what some classes in use are rather than assume magic.

Okay, I'll make some changes and explain why they are necessary. Here's a line of code it's complaining about:

```
if (($result->home_score + $result->away_score) >= 13)
```

PHPStan is looking at this and saying. "I'm not 100% sure what could be in `$result->home_score` or `$result->away_score` so can you clear things up?"

I think that is a fair question. A revised line could look like this:

```
if ((int)($result->home_score + $result->away_score) >= 13)
```

Another way to do it would be even stricter and cast both values to be integers.

```
if (((int) $result->home_score + (int) $result->away_score) >= 13)
```

A developer friend of mine has said on more than one occasion that code that uses static analysis tools "no longer looks like PHP." Which is to say, "It no longer looks like PHP code the way a lot of people write it." PHP is incredibly forgiving in many cases due to its dynamic typing capabilities. It tries to figure out what your intent is. Maybe those `home_score` and `away_score` class attributes are always going to be integers. By deliberately casting them as integers, I am 100% making sure that comparison does not cause a PHP-related error. Hopefully, those two attributes never have incorrect values!

So at level 2, it says there are four more errors. I'll fix the other math-related one and then turn my attention to those other reported problems.

```
 ------ -----------------------------------------------------------
  Line   src/Model/Table/GamesTable.php
 ------ -----------------------------------------------------------
  143    Call to an undefined method Cake\ORM\Query::orWhere().
 ------ -----------------------------------------------------------
```

This error is because PHPStan cannot understand where that `orWhere()` method comes from. Is this really an error? No. The code clearly works, so I could tell PHPStan to ignore this problem. According to the documentation I could add a PHPStan-specific annotation to tell it to ignore the error coming from that line.

Let's do that–some tools can definitely report false positives and I feel like this is one of them. This is what the updated code looks like now:

```
return $this->find()
    ->where(['week <=' => $week])
    ->contain('HomeTeams, AwayTeams', function (Query $q) use ($teams) {
    /** @phpstan-ignore-next-line */
        return $q->where('HomeTeams in', $teams)
            ->orWhere('AwayTeams in', $teams);
    });
```

Down to just two errors. The next one is this:

```
------ --------------------------------------------------------------------------
 Line   src/Util/Rosters.php
------ --------------------------------------------------------------------------
 15     Call to an undefined method Cake\ORM\Table::generateListByNicknameName().
------ --------------------------------------------------------------------------
```

Hrm. I did a search of the codebase, and that method doesn't exist at all. Is this dead code? An experiment I was doing and never finished? More searching makes me believe that it is, in fact, code that is not being used. Manual testing of the page that displays rosters verifies this is the case.

Okay, down to one last error:

```
------ ------------------------------------------------------------
 Line   src/View/AjaxView.php
------ ------------------------------------------------------------
 48     Call to an undefined method Cake\Http\Response::type().
------ ------------------------------------------------------------
```

I suspect this is code that older versions of the framework used, but along the upgrade path, it's stuck around. I could delete the file, but I do not have enough test coverage to feel comfortable doing it. Instead, I am going to add some details to the `phpstan.neon` file that tells it to ignore this file.

```
parameters:
    bootstrapFiles:
        - config/bootstrap.php
    level: 2
    paths:
        - src
        - tests
    excludePaths:
        analyse:
            - src/View
```

No more errors! I have to increase the analysis level to six before I get another set of problems to review:

```
Note: Using configuration file /Users/chartjes/Sites/ibl/phpstan.neon.
 48/48 [▓▓▓▓▓▓▓▓▓▓▓▓▓▓▓▓▓▓▓▓▓▓▓▓▓▓▓▓] 100%

 ------ -------------------------------------------------------------------
  Line   src/Model/Table/GamesTable.php
 ------ -------------------------------------------------------------------
  143    Method App\Model\Table\GamesTable::findAllByTeams() has parameter $teams with no value type specified in iterable type array.
         □ See: https://phpstan.org/blog/solving-phpstan-no-value-type-specified-in-iterable-type
  143    Method App\Model\Table\GamesTable::findAllByTeams() return type has no value type specified in iterable type Cake\ORM\Query.
         □ See: https://phpstan.org/blog/solving-phpstan-no-value-type-specified-in-iterable-type
 ------ -------------------------------------------------------------------

 ------ -------------------------------------------------------------------
  Line   src/Model/Table/TeamsTable.php
 ------ -------------------------------------------------------------------
  104    Method App\Model\Table\TeamsTable::findByConference() return type has no value type specified in iterable type Cake\ORM\Query.
         □ See: https://phpstan.org/blog/solving-phpstan-no-value-type-specified-in-iterable-type
 ------ -------------------------------------------------------------------

 ------ -------------------------------------------------------------
  Line   src/Util/Boxscore.php
 ------ -------------------------------------------------------------
  12     Property App\Util\Boxscore::$schedule has no typehint specified.
  13     Property App\Util\Boxscore::$teams has no typehint specified.
  14     Property App\Util\Boxscore::$games has no typehint specified.
 ------ -------------------------------------------------------------


 [ERROR] Found 6 errors
```

Also, you now see PHPStan offering suggestions on how to solve some of the issues at this level. It seems like it is highlighting the same problem. I'll go and read the page that URL points to.

Okay, the first one:

```
 ------ -----------------------------------------------------------------------
  Line   src/Model/Table/GamesTable.php
 ------ -----------------------------------------------------------------------
  143    Method App\Model\Table\GamesTable::findAllByTeams() has parameter
$teams with no value type specified in iterable type array.
         □ See: https://phpstan.org/blog/solving-phpstan-no-value-type-speci-
fied-in-iterable-type
```

Here's the code it doesn't like:

```
    public function findAllByTeams(int $week, array $teams): Query
```

It wants to know what is inside `$teams`. I believe it is an integer, so I can create a docblock for that method, make sure to add that in there, and then I can re-run PHPStan.

```
    /**
     * @param int $week
     * @param array<int> $teams
     * @return Query
     */
    public function findAllByTeams(int $week, array $teams): Query
    {
        return $this->find()
            ->where(['week <=' => $week])
            ->contain('HomeTeams, AwayTeams', function (Query $q) use ($teams) {
            /** @phpstan-ignore-next-line */
                return $q->where('HomeTeams in', $teams)
                    ->orWhere('AwayTeams in', $teams);
            });
    }
```

The next problem PHPStan is complaining about is that it wants to know what is inside that `Query` collection the `findByAllTeams()` method is returning. The answer is to change the return type to say it is returning `GamesTable` objects in that `Query` collection. With that change, here's the whole method.

```
/**
 * @param int $week
 * @param array<int> $teams
 * @return Query<GamesTable>
 */
public function findAllByTeams(int $week, array $teams): Query
{
    return $this->find()
        ->where(['week <=' => $week])
        ->contain('HomeTeams, AwayTeams', function (Query $q) use ($teams) {
        /** @phpstan-ignore-next-line */
            return $q->where('HomeTeams in', $teams)
                ->orWhere('AwayTeams in', $teams);
        });
}
```

So what was the point of this other than just making PHPStan happy? As mentioned earlier in this chapter, many IDEs can look at those document blocks and the code itself and make code completion easier. If other code is iterating over the collection of objects being returned by that method, it can verify what methods are available on those objects.

All of this static analysis has one goal–code that is clearer in intent, easier to debug, and less likely to behave in unexpected ways.

There are only two more sets of errors left at this level. I want to fix this one:

```
------ --------------------------------------------------------------------
  Line   src/Model/Table/TeamsTable.php
 ------ -------------------------------------------------------------------
  104    Method App\Model\Table\TeamsTable::findByConference() return type has
no value type specified in iterable type Cake\ORM\Query.
         □ See: https://phpstan.org/blog/solving-phpstan-no-value-type-speci-
fied-in-iterable-type
 ------ -------------------------------------------------------------------
```

This is a similar issue to the one I just fixed. Similar solution:

```
/**
 * @param string $conference
 * @return Query<TeamsTable>
 */
public function findByConference(string $conference): Query
{
    return $this->find()
        ->contain('Divisions')
        ->where(['Divisions.conference' => $conference]);
}
```

One last set of problems to fix!

```
------ ------------------------------------------------------------
 Line   src/Util/Boxscore.php
------ ------------------------------------------------------------
 12     Property App\Util\Boxscore::$schedule has no typehint specified.
 13     Property App\Util\Boxscore::$teams has no typehint specified.
 14     Property App\Util\Boxscore::$games has no typehint specified.
------ ------------------------------------------------------------
```

Just missing some type hints. Looking at the code, I know what type it should be. The updated code should look like this:

```php
<?php

declare(strict_types=1);

namespace App\Util;

use Cake\ORM\Locator\TableLocator;
use Cake\ORM\Table;

class Boxscore
{
    public Table $games;
    public Table $schedule;
    public Table $teams;


    public function __construct()
    {
        $this->schedule = (new TableLocator())->get('Schedule');
        $this->teams = (new TableLocator())->get('Teams');
        $this->games = (new TableLocator())->get('Games');
    }

```

```
    /**
     * @param int $slackerWeek
     * @return array<string, mixed>
     */
    public function getMissing(int $slackerWeek): array
    {
        if ($slackerWeek === 0) {
            return [];
        }

        $missingBoxes = [];

        // Build an array of teams with codes
        $results = $this->teams->fin()
            ->select(['ibl', 'code'])
            ->all();
        $teams = [];

        foreach ($results as $result) {
            $teams[$result->code] = $result->ibl;
        }

        $results = $this->schedule
            ->find()
            ->contain('Teams')
            ->where(['Schedule.status' => 0, 'Schedule.week <=' =>
$slackerWeek])
            ->order('Schedule.week, Teams.ibl');

        foreach ($results as $result) {
            $key = $result->week . $teams[$result->home];
            $missingBoxes[$key] = "wk{$result->week} {$teams[$result-
>away]}@{$teams[$result->home]}";
        }

        ksort($missingBoxes, SORT_NATURAL);
        return $missingBoxes;
    }
}
```

Now I set the PHPStan analysis level to 7 and see what problems it reports.

```
------ ---------------------------------------------------------------------
 Line   src/Console/Installer.php
------ ---------------------------------------------------------------------
 148    Parameter #1 $array of function array_diff expects array, array<int,
string>|false given.
 180    Parameter #3 $subject of function str_replace expects array|string,
string|false given.
------ ---------------------------------------------------------------------
```

This is code I didn't write; it was created by the framework. I'll tell PHPStan to ignore it.

```
parameters:
    bootstrapFiles:
        - config/bootstrap.php
    level: 7
    paths:
        - src
        - tests
    excludePaths:
        analyse:
            - src/View
            - src/Console/Installer.php

```

The final result is that PHPStan no longer complains about anything!

Bonus Round!

PHPStan revealed a small number of problems with the codebase. What if you have a much less-structured application? I happen to have one like that too! There is another application that could be considered a "companion" to the one I have been sharing samples from. It has almost no structure to it at all. Let's say I want to start applying static analysis to this codebase at its highest level. What would it say?

The first step is to create a PHPStan configuration file:

```
parameters:
    bootstrapFiles:
        - vendor/autoload.php
    level: 7
    paths:
        - .
    excludePaths:
        analyse:
            - vendor
```

How bad could it be?

```
[ERROR] Found 312 errors
```

Maybe that's pretty bad. Now, chances are that if this was some kind of paid project instead of a hobbyist one I might not want to spend all that developer time fixing older problems. Instead, I want to make sure all new code I write can be analyzed by PHPStan but accept the current state of the codebase.

For this, PHPStan has the concept of "setting a baseline." Using the `--generate-baseline` switch from the command line, PHPStan generates a file that contains all the errors it finds.

Here's what I saw when I ran that command:

```
./vendor/bin/phpstan --generate-baseline

Note: Using configuration file /Users/chartjes/ibl.dev/webreg/phpstan.neon.
 64/64 [▓▓▓▓▓▓▓▓▓▓▓▓▓▓▓▓▓▓▓▓▓▓▓▓▓▓▓▓] 100%



 [OK] Baseline generated with 312 errors
```

Then, according to the instructions, I add a reference to this file in my `phpstan.neon` configuration file.

```
includes:
    - phpstan-baseline.neon

parameters:
    bootstrapFiles:
        - vendor/autoload.php
    level: 7
    paths:
        - .
    excludePaths:
        analyse:
            - vendor
```

Having done this, I should not see any errors the next time I ask PHPStan to analyze my code:

```
Note: Using configuration file /Users/chartjes/ibl.dev/webreg/phpstan.neon.
 64/64 [▓▓▓▓▓▓▓▓▓▓▓▓▓▓▓▓▓▓▓▓▓▓▓▓▓▓▓▓] 100%



 [OK] No errors
```

Now I can start refactoring or adding code to the project, and PHPStan will only report on errors it hasn't already seen. This is a very handy tool for large legacy projects.

Chapter 3

Mutation Testing

What Is It?

Have you ever wondered if there was a way to test the tests you've been writing? That is essentially what mutation testing is.

My preferred tool for doing mutation testing in PHP is Infection[1], and it defines mutation testing as:

> Mutation testing involves modifying a program in small ways. Each mutated version is called a Mutant. To assess the quality of a given test set, these mutants are executed against the input test set to see if the seeded faults can be detected. If mutated program produces failing tests, this is called a killed mutant. If tests are green with mutated code, then we have an escaped mutant.

In the case of Infection, it works together with PHPUnit to make informed random changes to the code, and then execute the test.

---

[1] *Infection: https://infection.github.io*

Why Should I Use It?

My approach to writing unit tests goes something like this:

- What is the scenario I am writing a test for?
- What are my dependencies?
- How do I create those dependencies?
- How do I give those dependencies to the code I am testing?
- What assertions do I need to make?
- Does any code need to change to make those assertions succeed?

If I come up with enough scenarios, I start to take it for granted that I have both sufficient test coverage and that the tests themselves are good.

Mutation testing sets about to challenge that second assumption. If it mutates your code by doing something like switching `if ($foo > $bar)` to `if ($foo < bar)` and a test for that portion of code still passes, there is a problem with your test.

Yes, sometimes tests succeed by accident! If you are making heavy use of test doubles, you need a way to detect whether the code you are creating doubles for behaves the way the test expects. Otherwise, you end up with tests that pass but no longer reflect how the code actually works.

How Do I Use It?

In our sample app, I wanted to create a test for some code which verifies that the ordering of teams in our standings works correctly. The test looks like this:

```
    public function it_sorts_standings_correctly(): void
    {
        $unsortedStandings = unserialize(
            (string) file_get_contents(__DIR__ . '/../../../Fixture/unSortedStandings.txt')
        );
        $expectedStandings = unserialize(
            (string) file_get_contents(__DIR__ . '/../../../Fixture/sortedStandings.txt')
        );

        $results = $this->component->sort($unsortedStandings);

        self::assertSame($expectedStandings['AC'], $results);
    }
```

This seems like a straightforward test. Can mutation testing reveal that our expectations are wrong?

Before we can get to that point, there was some configuration work I had to do. First, I needed to create the configuration file for Infection itself. It's named `infection.json` and stored in the root directory for the project:

```
{
    "source": {
        "directories": [
            "src",
            "templates"
        ]
    },
    "logs" {
        "text": "infection.log"
    },
    "mutators": {
        "@default": true
    },
    "tmpDir": "tmp",
    "testFramework": "phpunit"
}
```

Next, I made sure I had my PHPUnit configuration file set up the way I wanted it. It's named `phpunit.xml` and it goes in the root directory for the project as well:

```
<phpunit bootstrap="tests/bootstrap.php">
    <listeners>
        <listener class="\Cake\TestSuite\Fixture\FixtureInjector">
            <arguments>
                <object class="\Cake\TestSuite\Fixture\FixtureManager" />
            </arguments>
        </listener>
    </listeners>
    <testsuites>
        <testsuite name="unit">
            <directory>tests</directory>
        </testsuite>
    </testsuites>
</phpunit>
```

The framework I am using provided the `bootstrap.php` file for me. Check the documentation for your framework for more details, or if you are using a custom solution, you'll have to figure out what should belong in that file.

With those two configuration files in place, I used Infection's `--filter=/path/to/code/to/test` CLI option to tell it what code we are looking at. So what were the results of running it?

```
php infection.phar --filter=src/Controller/Component/StandingsComponent.php

Running initial test suite...

PHPUnit version: 8.5.15

   23 [============================] 8 secs

Generate mutants...

Processing source code files: 1/1
.: killed, M: escaped, U: uncovered, E: fatal error, T: timed out, S: skipped

UUUUUUT..............MMMMMMMMMMMMMMMMMMMMMMMMMMMMM   ( 50 / 302)
MMMMMMMMMMMMMMMMMMMMMMMMMMMMMMMMMMMMMMM.M.........   (100 / 302)
M...MMMMMMMMMMMMMMMMMMTMMMMMMMMMMMMMMMMMMMMMMMMMMM   (150 / 302)
MMMMMMMMMMM..M..MMMMMMMMMMMMM.MMM..MMMMMMMMMMMMMMM   (200 / 302)
MMMMMM.MMMMMMMMMMMMMMMMMMMMMMMMMMMMMMMMMMMMMMMMMMM   (250 / 302)
MMMMMMMMMMMMMMMMMMMMMM..MMMMMMMMMMMMMMMMMMMMMMMMM.   (300 / 302)
.M                                                   (302 / 302)

302 mutations were generated:
      39 mutants were killed
       6 mutants were not covered by tests
     255 covered mutants were not detected
       0 errors were encountered
       2 time outs were encountered
       0 mutants required more time than configured

Metrics:
         Mutation Score Indicator (MSI): 13%
         Mutation Code Coverage: 98%
         Covered Code MSI: 13%

Please note that some mutants will inevitably be harmless (i.e. false positives).

Time: 4m 33s. Memory: 0.03GB
```

To be completely transparent: the code I was asking it to look at has pretty much no automated tests other than the one that checks the sorting and some functional-style tests that check whether content shows up on the page where I expect.

What information in that summary should we be worried about? Because we don't have 100% code coverage for `StandingsComponent.php`, it's hard to come up with a good answer. What answers the tool provides can lead us toward figuring out where to focus our attention.

Mutation Score Indicator (MSI)

You want this value to be as high as possible. It represents the percentage of mutations that were caught by your tests. To understand what this means, the process is like this:

- change something in the code you are analyzing
- run the tests that "cover" that code
- if the tests still pass, you have a mutant that was not caught

13% is a very low number and represents that our existing tests did not find most of the mutations, meaning our tests happily passed despite changes that should've been found. Not great!

Mutation Code Coverage

This value should be close to your existing code coverage. I have no idea what my current code coverage is, but seeing that it is 98% is very interesting. Given the spread between this value and the MSI, it means I need a lot more tests.

Covered Code Mutation Score Indicator

This is the value to really look at – it shows what the MSI is for code that was actually covered by tests. Now, because I filtered things out and told Infection to only look at one file, this should map exactly to the MSI. Again, this number is really low.

Logging Of Mutants

In my configuration file, I asked Infection to write what it was doing to a file called `infection.log`, which is being written into the root directory of our application. Because I only really have that one test for the sorting method, let me search for any mutations that were done to that code:

```
66) /workspace/src/Controller/Component/StandingsComponent.php:192    [M]
Foreach_

--- Original
+++ New
@@ @@
     public function sort(array $standings) : array
     {
         $column = [];
-        foreach ($standings as $tmp) {
+        foreach (array() as $tmp) {
             $column[] = $tmp['pct'];
         }
         array_multisort($column, SORT_DESC, $standings);


67) /workspace/src/Controller/Component/StandingsComponent.php:196    [M]
FunctionCallRemoval

--- Original
+++ New
@@ @@
         foreach ($standings as $tmp) {
             $column[] = $tmp['pct'];
         }
-        array_multisort($column, SORT_DESC, $standings);
+
         // Determine who is the leader for games behind
         $leaderDiff = 0;
         foreach ($standings as $info) {
```

If you're not familiar with the notation here, it is following what you would be seeing if you were using a version control system or a tool that can show you differences between two files (more commonly known as a "diff" tool).

The first mutant changed a foreach loop that was grabbing details about a column we wanted to sort by.

The second mutant removed a sorting of an array altogether.

How did those tests pass with those changes!? I can apply one of those myself and see if the test passes.

It does (which I don't understand), but it also reports a bunch of notices:

```
Notice Error: Trying to access array offset on value of type null
```

What I don't understand is: How can this test still pass!?!? Am I doing the wrong comparison? Is there something wrong with my test?

First, I check to make sure that right from the beginning, my unsorted data does not match the sorted data.

```
public function it_sorts_standings_correctly(): void
    {
        $unsortedStandings = unserialize(
            (string) file_get_contents(__DIR__ . '/../../../Fixture/
unSortedStandings.txt')
        );
        $expectedStandings = unserialize(
            (string) file_get_contents(__DIR__ . '/../../../Fixture/
sortedStandings.txt')
        );

        self::assertNotEquals($unsortedStandings, $expectedStandings['AC']);

        $results = $this->component->sort($unsortedStandings);

        self::assertEquals($expectedStandings['AC'], $results);
    }
```

That assertion failed. There's bad data in those fixtures! The next step is to fix that and make sure the two fixtures are actually different.

Next, I run that same test case again, and it passes, meaning I actually have different data. I run Infection again, and things improved...slightly.

```
        Mutation Score Indicator (MSI): 14%
        Mutation Code Coverage: 98%
        Covered Code MSI: 14%
```

It's time to go look at the output log for clues as to what mutants are making it past my one existing test.

```
67) /workspace/src/Controller/Component/StandingsComponent.php:202    [M] DecrementInteger

--- Original
+++ New
@@ @@
         }
         array_multisort($column, SORT_DESC, $standings);
         // Determine who is the leader for games behind
-        $leaderDiff = 0;
+        $leaderDiff = -1;
         foreach ($standings as $info) {
             $zVal = $info['w'] - $info['l'];
             if ($zVal > $leaderDiff) {


68) /workspace/src/Controller/Component/StandingsComponent.php:207    [M] GreaterThan

--- Original
+++ New
@@ @@
         $leaderDiff = 0;
         foreach ($standings as $info) {
             $zVal = $info['w'] - $info['l'];
-            if ($zVal > $leaderDiff) {
+            if ($zVal >= $leaderDiff) {
                 $leaderDiff = $zVal;
             }
         }
```

Those are the only two dealing with the `sort` method our latest test deals with. As before, I am modifying the source directly to see whether the test fails as it should. The test still passes. The next question to be asked is, "Does this actually matter?" Some mutants are actually false positives.

In the case of Mutant 67, the answer to why it is a false positive can be found in Mutant 68. If the condition comparing `$zVal` to `$leaderDiff` is met, I overwrite what value goes into `$leaderDiff`, so having that value start at -1 might be incorrect, but it does not cause the test to fail.

Mutant 68 is a more interesting one. Under what circumstances would it matter if that conditional statement changed? Given how I am calculating the number of "games behind" for a team, I don't think it really matters at all. This one can be considered a false positive.

When Should I Use Mutation Testing?

As I showed in the section above, the best time to use mutation testing is during development. It can be used as a tool to guide you towards creating better tests by examining any "escape mutants" to see if there is anything that can be done.

In my case, I had an invalid test to begin with. See, it even happens to experienced developers! Taking a look at the mutants and applying the change myself sent me down the path towards fixing a broken test.

I would not run mutation testing as part of any continuous integration build system. The fact that it can return false positives means it could cause a failing build for no reason.

Much like static code analysis tools, it is an excellent tool for getting your testing to that "next level" status. Having tests is good; having effective tests is even better!

Chapter 4

Linting and Formatting Your Code

The first time I came across a programming language that came "out of the box" with a code formatter was when I first played around With Go[1] more than a decade ago. I was equally shocked to see how the Go community embraced it so quickly. Given all the online arguments I had seen over the years about things like semicolon usage in JavaScript and where to put opening and closing braces in PHP, it felt like a small breath of fresh air to see it.

Over the years, I discovered code linters and formatters can do a lot more than tell you "that opening brace is in the wrong place." They can enforce many practices that often come up in code reviews and can also be used in build systems to apply those changes for you. An OSS project I used to lead made heavy use of them in ways that would surprise you.

---

[1] Go: https://golang.org/

What

Linters and formatters are usually CLI tools that can be run locally by developers. Many IDEs also have integrations for using them. Learn your IDE inside and out! It can help automate a lot of the repetitive work that makes up so much of coding.

These tools analyze your code, usually based on a customizable set of rules, and identify where these rules have not been followed. Formatters are often combined with a linter and use the same concept of configurable rules to identify and then modify the code.

The strength of them being run via a CLI is that they can also be used as part of any continuous integration or build service.

Why

A concept I have tried to instill in other developers over the years is that we should ask the computer to do any repetitive tasks for us. That way (or so my theory goes), we can stop worrying about those tasks and use our mental energy to solve other problems.

The ability to enforce a coding standard or even the use of specific language constructs means you have code that is consistent across the entire application. That consistency, in turn, tends to speed up comprehension, debugging, and often allows you to introduce other tools that are expecting your code to look and behave in a specific way.

Given that some linters and formatters can insert copyright documentation blocks or even tell you that you are missing a unit test for that code (yes, that is something that can be done), why would you not want to have what is essentially an on-call coworker who can point out (and more importantly) fix problems that might not have surfaced until code review time?

How

Much like my recommendations for testing frameworks, editors, static code analyzers, and operating systems–pick one that does the job you need it to and go from there. There is no perfect tool for this!

For my own projects, I advocate using Easy Coding Standard[2] as it allows you to use definitions created by other tools. As I write this book, I am using version 9.3.12.

---

[2] *Easy Coding Standard: https://github.com/symplify/easy-coding-standard*

I have also used PHP_CodeSniffer[3] and PHP CS Fixer[4] and code linters and fixers in other languages; my preference was to use Black[5] for the Python code I wrote at Mozilla. Again, it doesn't really matter what one you use.

How can we actually use this? I borrow a PHP CS Fixer ruleset from another project and get it to play nicely with ECS. There is some great documentation from the ECS project pointing to blog posts about how others converted rulesets.

For my first pass, I told it to:

- enforce short array syntax
- enforce PSR12[6]
- only apply it to my `src` and `tests` directories

Here is what the `ecs.php` configuration file looks like:

```
<?php

declare(strict_types=1);

use PhpCsFixer\Fixer\ArrayNotation\ArraySyntaxFixer;
use Symfony\Component\DependencyInjection\Loader\Configurator\ContainerConfigurator;
use Symplify\EasyCodingStandard\ValueObject\Option;
use Symplify\EasyCodingStandard\ValueObject\Set\SetList;

return static function (ContainerConfigurator $containerConfigurator): void {
    $parameters = $containerConfigurator->parameters();
    $parameters->set(Option::PATHS, [
        __DIR__ . '/src',
        __DIR__ . '/tests',
    ]);

    $services = $containerConfigurator->services();
    $services->set(ArraySyntaxFixer::class)
        ->call('configure', [[
            'syntax' => 'short',
        ]]);
    $containerConfigurator->import(SetList::PSR_12);

};
```

[3] *PHP_CodeSniffer: https://github.com/squizlabs/PHP_CodeSniffer*
[4] *PHP CS Fixer: https://github.com/FriendsOfPhp/PHP-CS-Fixer*
[5] *Black: https://github.com/psf/black*
[6] *PSR12: https://www.php-fig.org/psr/psr-12/*

Time to let it run and tell me what it found!

```
[WARNING] 42 errors are fixable! Just add "--fix" to console command and rerun
to apply.
```

That is not surprising given the age of the codebase. The next step is to tell the tool to fix all those changes for me.

```
./vendor/bin/ecs check --fix
```

It does all the work, and here's an example of one of the changes it made for me:

```
42) tests/TestCase/Util/BoxscoreTest.php

    ---------- begin diff ----------
--- Original
+++ New
@@ -1,4 +1,5 @@
 <?php
+
 declare(strict_types=1);

 use App\Model\Table\GamesTable;
@@ -12,9 +13,9 @@
     public function it_finds_missing_boxscores(): void
     {
         /** @var GamesTable $games */
-        $games = (new TableLocator)->get('Games');
+        $games = (new TableLocator())->get('Games');

-        $results = (new Boxscore)->getMissing($games->getMaxWeek());
+        $results = (new Boxscore())->getMissing($games->getMaxWeek());

         if (count($results) === 0) {
             self::markTestSkipped('No missing boxscores available');
    ----------- end diff -----------


Applied checkers:

 * PhpCsFixer\Fixer\Operator\NewWithBracesFixer
 * PhpCsFixer\Fixer\PhpTag\BlankLineAfterOpeningTagFixer



 [OK] 42 errors successfully fixed and no other errors found!
```

See, now the tool does all the things I either did not know were part of the PSR-12 standard, or things I keep forgetting to do myself.

Hrm. I notice my files don't all have a `declare(strict_types=1);` statement. Could we add that as a rule?

Looking in the documentation I see that there is a rule for it:

```
$services->set(DeclareStrictTypesFixer::class);
```

I add this to my `ecs.php` file, and away it goes.

```

All sorts of output snipped...

31) tests/bootstrap.php

    ---------- begin diff ----------
--- Original
+++ New
@@ -1,4 +1,6 @@
 <?php
+
+declare(strict_types=1);
 /**
  * Test runner bootstrap.
  *
    ----------- end diff -----------


Applied checkers:

 * PhpCsFixer\Fixer\PhpTag\BlankLineAfterOpeningTagFixer
 * PhpCsFixer\Fixer\Strict\DeclareStrictTypesFixer



 [WARNING] 31 errors are fixable! Just add "--fix" to console command and rerun to apply.
```

Great; it's a quick fix, and I don't have to worry about that any more.

Now I check to make sure I haven't broken anything... and my tests show some errors! Both in one file that did not have strict typing in it. Two changes later (casting variables to expected values), and my test suite is passing again! What else can it do?

How about saving us from remembering to order our imports?

```
    $services->set(OrderedImportsFixer::class);
```

```
1) src/Model/Table/GamesTable.php

    ---------- begin diff ----------
--- Original
+++ New
@@ -6,8 +6,8 @@

 use Cake\ORM\Association\BelongsTo;
 use Cake\ORM\Locator\TableLocator;
+use Cake\ORM\Query;
 use Cake\ORM\Table;
-use Cake\ORM\Query;

 /**
  * Games Model
    ----------- end diff -----------


Applied checkers:

 * PhpCsFixer\Fixer\Import\OrderedImportsFixer
```

I want all my PHPUnit tests to use an annotation to indicate a method is a test case instead of prepending test:

```
    $services->set(PhpUnitTestAnnotationFixer::class)
        ->call('configure', [[
            'style' => 'annotation'
        ]]);
```

```
3) tests/TestCase/Model/Table/GamesTableTest.php

    ---------- begin diff ----------
--- Original
+++ New
@@ -15,7 +15,10 @@
   */
 class GamesTableTest extends TestCase
 {
-    public function testGetWeeklyResult(): void
+    /**
+     * @test
+     */
+    public function getWeeklyResult(): void
     {
         /** @var GamesTable $table */
         $table = (new TableLocator())->get('Games');
    ----------- end diff -----------


Applied checkers:

 * PhpCsFixer\Fixer\PhpUnit\PhpUnitTestAnnotationFixer
```

When

In my experience, there are three places to use code linters and formatters:

During Development

The most common practice if it is not mandatory for a particular project is to have the developers use the linting and formatting tools during their work and hopefully before committing and pushing their code for review or merging.

I have done this on projects where these tools were not mandatory.

Before Version Control Usage

If you are using a version control system that has the concept of a "pre-commit hook," I highly recommend reading the documentation for your VCS on how to use them and set one up.

This way, if you have forgotten to run the linter it will be done before your VCS tooling pushes your code to the repository.

During Builds or Continuous Integration

This is my preferred time to have linting tools run, with any problems being reported by the linter being considered a failed build. Again, this also relies on you having a build system or continuous integration system you can customize to run arbitrary commands from the command line.

If you are using something like GitHub Actions[7] you can find examples of how to do it. In a later chapter of this book where I show some examples of using continuous integration systems, you can probably figure out where to add a linting step.

---

[7] GitHub Actions: https://github.com/features/actions

Chapter 5

Continuous Integration

I am a big fan of getting computers to do repetitive actions for me. It frees up my attention to focus on solving other problems instead of remembering a series of steps where missing one can result in failure.

One of the issues most programming projects face is coming up with a way to integrate code changes with the least amount of friction. There is no way to do it without any kind of pain and effort either on the development side or the tool creation side.

As I write this in the spring of 2021, there are two dominant methods of integrating your code. The first I call "integrate into main with flags" and "integrate via pull-request."

Integrate Via Pull Request

With a large percentage of developers making use of GitHub (ironically a set of centralized web-based tools for a distributed version control system) most of the folks reading this are familiar with the use of the "pull request."

For those not familiar, here's a high-level explanation:

A developer creates a branch of the code under version control and does some work in that branch. Once they are ready to share, they use tooling to create a "pull request," which is a notification that there are some changes to be reviewed. Generally speaking, you are comparing the developer's work in their own branch with the main branch that gets deployed into a production environment.

People reviewing the pull request can see what the changes are and make comments about those changes. One of the downsides of the pull request method is that long-running work can easily get out of date if the codebase itself is changing rapidly. This, in turn, forces the developer to do a lot of work, constantly merging in other changes from other developers that have been applied to the main branch.

This method puts the pressure for smooth integrations onto the tooling by providing tools that reduce the friction involved in managing all these changes.

Integrate Via Flags

As more people experience some of the pains and frustrations of a pull-request-centric integration plan, other programmers have been advocating not using separate branches for their work. Instead, they work in the main branch that is deployed and use "feature flags" or other techniques to make sure that the new code is only used under specific conditions.

Feature flags or other ways of configuring what code is available to users can be as complicated as an admin system where you define these values or as straight-forward as a conditional statement around a block of code.

The project I am using in this book does more of an "integrate with main" strategy, with a few flags to change what gets displayed. The other developer who helps out does pull requests for their work as they do not understand the codebase as well as I do.

This method puts the integration pressure on the developers to make sure the conditions under which this code should be executed are correct.

No matter what method you choose to use, the process for doing either method is well-established, and there are lots of resources available that can show how to do it.

Automating Integration and Testing

Local Automation

One of the reasons I so strongly advocate for automated tests of critical features of web applications is that the integrate-and-then-deploy process can be very stressful, especially in environments where parts of the deployment process are manual.

The one common trait of places where every deployment-to-production was stressful was a lack of tests to act as that first line of defense against integrations that might have gone wrong. Yes, I know it can often be difficult to wrap tests around legacy applications. For me, it is worth it because it increases confidence that any given deployment is going to work as expected.

Once there are some tests in place, you then need to start thinking about all the steps required to get to the final step of "did my tests pass?" In the case of the project being used in this book, it looks a little like this:

1. Pull in any changes from GitHub and apply them to my work.
2. Create a fresh test database and seed it with data.
3. Run `composer install` to have expected dependencies in place.
4. Run my tests.

If the tests pass, then I do a manual deployment of the changes on the production server for the application.

What if I wanted to automate this? First, I would create something that does it locally with one command. For projects using Composer, I can add things to a `scripts` section of the `composer.json` file.

But first, I'll create a bash[1] script with all the steps I need in it. I am leery of adding a step that automatically merges changes from the main branch because it might require me to fix conflicts or solve other Git-related issues before I can run my tests.

```
#!/usr/bin/env bash
PGPASSWORD=<redcated> psql -h 127.0.0.1 -U <redacted> ibl_stats_test < ibl_
stats.dump
composer install
vendor/bin/phpunit tests/
```

I've added this file to my project as `scripts/test-full.sh`.

For this project, I grab frequent snapshots of the production database and use them locally to always reset my test database to a known state. I then use Postgres' CLI tools to import that snapshot. Next, I install all my project dependencies, followed by running my tests.

I've verified that it runs locally and that my tests currently pass at the end.

[1] bash: https://www.gnu.org/software/bash/

The next step is to update our `composer.json` file so this script can be executed with the command `composer test-full`. I've added this after the last thing currently defined in there:

```
"scripts": {
        "test-full": "scripts/test-full.sh"
    }
```

I've verified that the command `composer test-full` now runs the bash script I created. I can now do all this work with just one command.

Build Servers

Ideally, I want to also have these steps followed by an automated system. Systems like this are often referred to as "build servers" or "continuous integration" servers. Regardless of the name, it is a system that executes a series of user-defined commands based on an event or trigger.

My first exposure to continuous integration systems was via learning how to use Jenkins[2] to run tests for a fantasy sports platform's Python code that handled generating all the points for participants. Jenkins is still a good choice for folks looking to get into automation surrounding your build-and-deploy process.

These days, I use GitHub Actions[3] to do this kind of work. With every single one of my coding projects using GitHub, it makes sense to take advantage of the integrations they provide.

Because GitHub Actions are language-agnostic, you have to tell it to do a lot of the configuration work and package installation you've done already just to get your local development environment up and running.

Their documentation is really good; I encourage you to read it to understand what is going on. Here is the GitHub Actions configuration file for my project. Don't worry, I will explain what is going on:

---

[2] *Jenkins: https://www.jenkins.io/*

[3] *GitHub Actions: https://github.com/features/actions*

```yaml
name: Grumpy CI
on: [push, pull_request]
jobs:
  CI:
    runs-on: ubuntu-latest
    services:
      postgres:
        image: postgres:10.8
        env:
          POSTGRES_USER: <redacted>
          POSTGRES_PASSWORD: <redacted>
          POSTGRES_DB: ibl_stats_test
        ports:
          - 5432:5432
        options: --health-cmd pg_isready --health-interval 10s --health-timeout 5s --health-retries 3
    steps:
      - name: Checkout
        uses: actions/checkout@v2
        with:
          lfs: true
      - name: Checkout LFS objects
        run: git lfs checkout
      - name: Setup PHP
        uses: shivammathur/setup-php@v2
        with:
          php-version: 7.4
          extensions: mbstring, intl, pdo_pgsql
      - name: Get composer cache directory
        id: composer-cache
        run: echo "::set-output name=dir::$(composer config cache-files-dir)"
      - name: Cache composer dependencies
        uses: actions/cache@v2
        with:
          path: ${{ steps.composer-cache.outputs.dir }}
          key: ${{ runner.os }}-composer-${{ hashFiles('**/composer.lock') }}
          restore-keys: ${{ runner.os }}-composer-
      - name: Install dependencies
        run:  composer install --no-progress --prefer-dist --optimize-autoloader
      - name: Seed DB
        run: PGPASSWORD=<redacted> psql -h 127.0.0.1 -U <redacted> ibl_stats_test < ibl_stats.dump
      - name: Run PHPUnit tests
        run: vendor/bin/phpunit tests
```

All this work happens inside some kind of containerized environment.

Starting at the top, I give this process a name and tell it I want it to react to any GitHub-related push event or pull request.

Next, I tell it that I want to use the latest available version of Ubuntu[4] Linux. GitHub installs some set of default packages as well. Adding other packages can be done in later steps.

With that defined, I have to declare I want to use one of their Postgres containers and specify some configuration values I need, along with adding an option for a health check that causes the whole process to pause until the Postgres container is up and running and ready to accept connections.

Then there are a series of steps I want to be followed. The first is to check out the code that is either being pushed or subject to a pull request.

The next step is unique to this project but might be of interest to you. Do you have large files (like, for instance, a Postgres database dump) that needs to be under version control? GitHub doesn't let you add files that large.

Luckily for me, when GitHub refused to accept a push that contained my database dump, it directed me to take a look at the Git Large File Storage[5] project and use that instead. After doing some repository reset and rewind work, I successfully added the database dump file to the repo. The file `ibl_stats.dump` is actually a text file that contains some metadata and a pointer to where the file can be downloaded.

With the files checked out, I ask for PHP to be installed, specifying the version and any other extensions to be installed.

Next, I find out where Composer's cache is, followed by telling Composer to, well, use that cache! After that, I install all of my composer-related dependencies.

I follow that up by doing some database seeding by applying the contents of that database dump to my freshly-created Postgres database.

The final step is to ask the build system to run my PHPUnit tests.

Now, I have GitHub following the same steps I follow locally so I can continue to integrate my code and, hopefully, have fewer bugs making it into production.

I hope you can use my sample GitHub Action file as a template for your own build systems. Basically, almost anything you find yourself doing just to get to the point where you can run your tests can be duplicated here.

---

[4] Ubuntu: https://ubuntu.com/
[5] Git Large File Storage: https://git-lfs.github.com/

Chapter 6

What's Next?

Like with almost everything associated with writing automated tests for your PHP code, it's a journey that won't stop. I learn new things all the time! My target goal for all of my work is this:

- Developers use TDD to create or update features.
- CI systems take their patches and run a comprehensive test suite against them.
- If all the tests pass, the patch is merged, and deployed to production.

Getting to this state can take a lot of work; some code bases and applications may never get there. However, we should never stop trying to use tools that encourage clear intent in code, alert us of problems before the users see them, and allow for confident deployments.

In this section, I wanted to talk briefly about some things I have noticed recently in regards to tools that complement testing. They don't need an entire chapter, but I think it's worth your time to dig in a little deeper.

Editor/IDE Integration

As mentioned before, I tend to use PhpStorm when doing PHP coding work. Out-of-the-box, it comes with a lot of tooling that makes writing PHP code easier. But its real strength is a plugin system that allows third parties to extend functionality and integration points to allow the use of CLI tools from inside the IDE.

If an external tool can be easily used within the IDE, spend the time to configure it. I like the ability to click a button to run a PHPUnit test case instead of always changing focus back to a terminal shell.

Reducing friction in your tooling is critical. I am always looking at how other developers accomplish similar tasks. Video pairing sessions where I watch people really leverage their tools are a great way to re-examine and evaluate what I am doing.

Containerized Development Environments

In my evaluation of Visual Studio Code[1] I was encouraged by long-time online friend Alvaro Videla[2] to take a look at the Remote Containers[3] extension, which provides the glue many other editors are missing to allow you to create and use containerized development environments using Docker[4]. It took me less than 30 minutes from reading the first bits of documentation to having a working development environment that works hand-in-hand with Visual Studio.

I also am aware you can do similar things with Docker and PhpStorm, but my own experiences were not as smooth as what Code provided. Making sure all developers on a project have a consistent, repeatable development environment can go a long way toward eliminating the "works for me" category of bugs.

[1] *Visual Studio Code: https://code.visualstudio.com/*
[2] *Alvaro Videla: https://twitter.com/old_sound*
[3] *Remote Containers: https://code.visualstudio.com/docs/remote/create-dev-container*
[4] *Docker: https://docker.com*

Made in United States
North Haven, CT
05 November 2026

21766909R00030